I Wonder Who
Stretched the Giraffe's Neck

Mona Gansberg Hodgson

**Illustrated by
Chris Sharp**

who...

SAINT LOUIS

For my nephew Micah.

I Wonder Series
I Wonder Who Hung the Moon in the Sky
I Wonder Who Stretched the Giraffe's Neck
I Wonder How Fish Sleep

Scripture quotations taken from the HOLY BIBLE, NEW INTERNATIONAL VERSION®. NIV®. Copyright © 1973, 1978, 1984 by International Bible Society. Used by permission of Zondervan Publishing House. All rights reserved.

Text copyright © 1999 Mona Gansberg Hodgson
Art copyright © 1999 Concordia Publishing House
Published by Concordia Publishing House
3558 S. Jefferson Avenue, St. Louis, MO 63118-3968
Manufactured in the United States of America

1   2   3   4   5   6   7   8   9   10   08   07   06   05   04   03   02   01   00   99

A Note to Parents and Teachers

The *I Wonder Series* will delight children while helping them grow in their understanding and appreciation of God. Readers will discover biblical truths through the experiences and whimsy of 7-year-old Jared.

This book, *I Wonder Who Stretched the Giraffe's Neck*, provides a playful exploration of God's creatures and His character while centering on scriptural truth. The activities on pages 30–32 will help children apply and practice the truths revealed in Jared's imaginative investigation of God's critter creations.

As you read this book together, share these Bible words with your child:

I will praise You, O LORD, with all my heart; I will tell of all Your wonders. Those who know Your name will trust in You, for You, LORD, have never forsaken those who seek You. *Psalm 9:1, 10*

Enjoy!

Mona Gansberg Hodgson

Hi! My name is Jared. I live in Arizona.

Do you wonder about things? I do. I wonder how animals know where to live. I wonder how a caterpillar turns into a butterfly. Everything makes me wonder.

-Ta-Da!

Some animals live on farms.

Some animals live in deserts.

Some animals live in jungles.

Who made all the animals?
I wonder.

$\mathcal{W}$ho put the bark in my dog, Chester? Who put the hop in rabbits? I wonder.

Do you ever wonder who made the animals?

My dad told me that God created the animals.

God made all the birds.
God made all the fish.

God made all the animals! That's a lot to make!

How did He create them all? I wonder.

Giraffes have the longest neck of any animal I can think of. Do you ever wonder who stretched the giraffe's neck? I wonder.

I think God gave them long necks so they can reach tall trees to munch leaves for lunch. What do you think?

- ahhh...

wls can twist their heads around. Why did God make owls that way? I wonder.

Papa Ray said God made owls able to twirl their heads so they can hunt from up in a tree. God takes care of everything!

Jackrabbits have really big ears. Do you think God gave them big ears so they can hear better? I wonder.

My mom said God made the jackrabbits' ears special to help keep them cool.

16

Where did zebras get their stripes? I wonder.

Do you think God painted the stripes on the zebras? My dad said, "God is so great He would not need paint to put the stripes on zebras. God can just speak and things happen."

Do you know the rooster's song? He crows, "Cock-a-doodle-do." Why did God give roosters a wake-up song? I wonder.

Papa Ray said God uses roosters to wake up the ranchers and the farmers. God thinks of everything!

21

Why do leopards have spots? I wonder.

I had spots when I had the chicken pox. Do you think leopards have the chicken pox? My dad said God put spots on leopards so they can hide in the jungle.

I saw a blue dragonfly. Why was it blue? I wonder.

Maybe God had some blue left over when He made the ocean so He splashed it on dragonflies. What do you think?

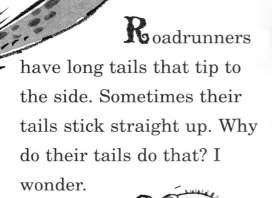

Roadrunners have long tails that tip to the side. Sometimes their tails stick straight up. Why do their tails do that? I wonder.

Mr. Adams

Mr. Adams said roadrunners use their tails to help them turn and to help them stop. God is so creative!

I like to wonder, don't you? When I wonder, I think about God. I like to think about God. I like to thank God for all the neat things He made.

I will praise You, O LORD, with all my heart; I will tell of all Your wonders. Those who know Your name will trust in You, for You, LORD, have never forsaken those who seek You. *Psalm 9:1, 10*

Thank You, God, for making all the
   animals.
Thank You, God, for making them so
   different from each other.
Thank You for being my amazing
   God! In the name of my Savior,
   Jesus Christ. Amen.

"God created a lot of neat animals. What are your favorite animals? Tell me about them in the space below."